D1712528

DIGITAL PLANET

WHAT IS CODING?

by Nikole Brooks Bethea

Ideas for Parents and Teachers

Pogo Books let children practice reading informational text while introducing them to nonfiction features such as headings, labels, sidebars, maps, and diagrams, as well as a table of contents, glossary, and index.

Carefully leveled text with a strong photo match offers early fluent readers the support they need to succeed.

Before Reading

- "Walk" through the book and point out the various nonfiction features. Ask the student what purpose each feature serves.
- Look at the glossary together. Read and discuss the words.

Read the Book

- Have the child read the book independently.
- Invite him or her to list questions that arise from reading.

After Reading

- Discuss the child's questions. Talk about how he or she might find answers to those questions.
- Prompt the child to think more. Ask: Did you know about coding before reading this book? What more would you like to learn after reading about it?

Pogo Books are published by Jump!
5357 Penn Avenue South
Minneapolis, MN 55419
www.jumplibrary.com

Library of Congress Cataloging-in-Publication Data

Names: Bethea, Nikole Brooks, author.
Title: What is coding? / by Nikole Brooks Bethea.
Description: Minneapolis, MN: Jump!, Inc., [2020]
Series: Digital planet
Audience: Ages 7 to 10. | Includes index.
Identifiers: LCCN 2019000134 (print)
LCCN 2019005731 (ebook)
ISBN 9781641288989 (ebook)
ISBN 9781641288965 (hardcover: alk. paper)
ISBN 9781641288972 (pbk.)
Subjects: LCSH: Computer programming—
Juvenile literature.
Classification: LCC QA76.6115 (ebook)
LCC QA76.6115 .B48 2020 (print)
DDC 005.1—dc23
LC record available at https://lccn.loc.gov/2019000134

Editor: Susanne Bushman
Designer: Michelle Sonnek
Content Consultant: Sarah McRoberts, Human-Computer Interaction Researcher

Photo Credits: Komkrit Noenpoempisut/Shutterstock, cover (background), 10 (computer); AlesiaKan/Shutterstock, cover (foreground); Asier Romero/Shutterstock, 1 (girl); In-Finity/Shutterstock, 1 (screen); artjazz/Shutterstock, 3 (computer); Heymo/Shutterstock, 3 (screen); Tony Stock/Shutterstock, 4 (boy); Chinnapong/Shutterstock, 4 (screen); Kojin/Shutterstock, 5; mirtmirt/Shutterstock, 6-7 (computer); BEST-BACKGROUNDS/Shutterstock, 6-7 (screen), 18-19 (screen); maicasaa/Shutterstock, 8-9; Kolonko/Shutterstock, 10 (screen), 20-21 (screen); Andrey_Popov/Shutterstock, 11, 15 (screen), 18-19 (background); Denys Prykhodov/Shutterstock, 12-13; Den Rozhnovsky/Shutterstock, 14 (computer); Anna Maloverjan/Shutterstock, 14 (screen); Veja/Shutterstock, 15 (tablet); Georgii Shipin/Shutterstock, 16-17; stockfour/Shutterstock, 20-21 (background); Photo_SS/Shutterstock, 23.

Printed in the United States of America at Corporate Graphics in North Mankato, Minnesota.

TABLE OF CONTENTS

CHAPTER 1

WHAT IS CODE?

Do you play video games or look at websites? Or use **apps**? **Code** runs these.

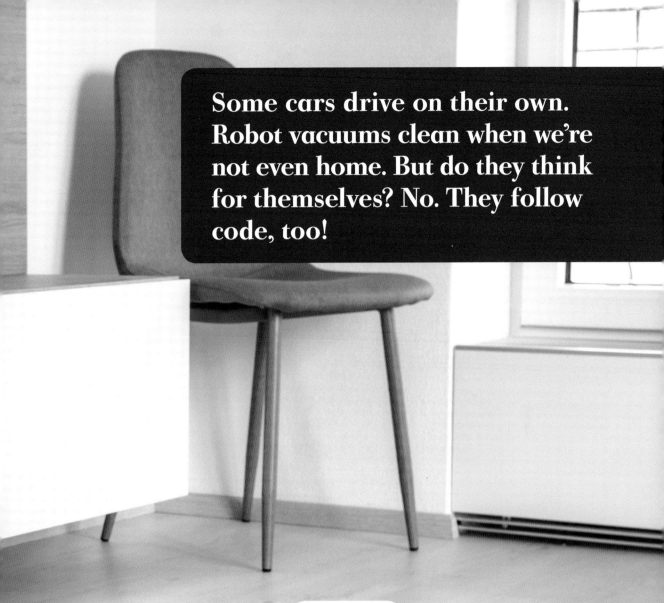

Some cars drive on their own. Robot vacuums clean when we're not even home. But do they think for themselves? No. They follow code, too!

vacuum

Code is typed in words. The words are step-by-step instructions. They are **translated** for a **device**. The code tells the device what to do.

```javascript
                    we.html(ye.unread_convs), ye.unread_convs ? we.addClass("unread-icon") :
                        we.removeClass("unread-icon")
                } else;
            if (ye.hasOwnProperty("unread_notifs"))
                if (ce.data.unread_notifs != ye.unread_notifs) {
                    ce.data.unread_notifs = ye.unread_notifs;
                    var we = $(".mmi-notif .hri-msg");
                    we.html(ye.unread_notifs), ye.unread_notifs ? we.addClass("unread-icon") :
                        we.removeClass("unread-icon")
                } else;
        })
    }

function J(ye) {
    if (ye.removeClass("inp_modified"), ye.hasClass("inp-field-select")) {
        var we = ye.find("select");
        if (we.length) {
            we.data("default") ? we.val(we.data("default")) : we.val("");
            var be = ye.find(".selectpicker");
            be.length && (we.data("default") ? be.selectpicker("val", we.data("default")) :
                be.selectpicker("val", "")), we.trigger("change")
        }
    } else if (ye.hasClass("inp-field-checkbox")) ye.find("input:checkbox").prop(
        "checked", !1).removeAttr("checked");
    else if (ye.hasClass("inp-field-range_slider")) {
        var ke = ye.find("#price_range"),
            xe = ke.bootstrapSlider("getAttribute", "min"),
```

code

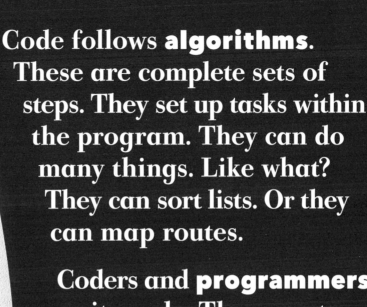

Code follows **algorithms**. These are complete sets of steps. They set up tasks within the program. They can do many things. Like what? They can sort lists. Or they can map routes.

Coders and **programmers** write code. They create **computer programs**. These are made of many algorithms!

DID YOU KNOW?

Code was once on paper! A card reader read holes in the paper. It sent the information to a computer.

CHAPTER 2

MANY LANGUAGES

There are hundreds of coding languages. Each one has rules. Coders use different words for each. Symbols and grammar change, too.

```
<script>
                var currentTime = new Date(),
    hours = currentTime.getHours(),
    minutes = currentTime.getMinutes();
                if (minutes < 10) {
                    minutes = "0" + minutes;
                }

                var suffix = "AM";
                if (hours >= 12) {
    suffix = "PM";
    hours = hours - 12;
```

symbol ····▶}

Each one can be used for many things. But they all have certain strengths. Like what? JavaScript is great for making website **animations**. C# works well for designing video games.

What are other languages? Python, Ruby, and PERL are some. Many fighter jets use C++. HTML is often used for websites. Facebook uses PHP.

DID YOU KNOW?

You can see a website's code. How? Right-click on the web page. Choose to view source. The code appears! Usually, it is in HTML.

CHAPTER 3

CODE TO COMPUTER

Computers can't understand coding languages. They have to be changed first. They become **binary code**. It is all 1s and 0s.

binary code

Unique sets of eight 1s and 0s stand for each letter, number, and symbol. Text and sound become binary code. Images and videos change, too.

Binary code is sent to a computer. **Circuits** help. They are inside computers on circuit boards. They are made of many **transistors**. These make on and off signals. That is all the computer understands! An on signal reads as a 1. An off signal reads as a 0. This is why binary code is only 1s and 0s.

circuit board

TAKE A LOOK!

What do numbers look like in binary code? Take a look!
Try writing your phone number in binary code!

Number	Binary Code
0	0011 0000
1	0011 0001
2	0011 0010
3	0011 0011
4	0011 0100
5	0011 0101
6	0011 0110
7	0011 0111
8	0011 1000
9	0011 1001

```
    var De = ce.lays.length;
    f(De - 1), B(De - 2), ce.lays.last().view
        Ie);
    var Re = ce.lays[De - 2].lay_id;
    $photoeditor_LAY = $("#lay_" + Re);
    var Se = "";
    $.each(ce.lays.last().views[0].photo_editor
        Se += editor_product_list_partial(Pe
    }), $photoeditor_LAY.find(".note-list").html
    ".note-list").tagDots({
    list_child: ".nli-item",
    value_x: "tagx",
    value_y: "tagy",
    common_container: ".my-photos-row",
    photo: ".mph-img-thumb",
    dot_tooltip: 0,
    after_ready: function() {
        $(".tag-dot-item").draggable()
    }
    })
} else Q({
    s7: Ae,
    handler_done: function(Ue) {
        var Pe = Ue.views[0].product_element;
        Pe.x = 1, Pe.y = 1;
        var Te = ce.lays.length;
        f(Te - 1), B(Te - 2), ce.lays.last().views[0].
        Pe), h(ce.lays[2].lay_id)
```

Binary code is long. It is too long for coders to use. They would need to use billions of 1s and 0s. This is why coders use coding languages. **Compilers** change it to binary code. Then the computer can read it.

The world needs coding. It can make new things. Coders could even make self-flying airplanes! More coders are needed. Would you like to learn coding?

```java
import java.util.Scanner;

public class EvenOdd {
    public static void main(

        Scanner reader = new

        System.out.print("En
        int num = reader.next

        if(num % 2 == 0)
            System.out.println
        else
            System.out.println
```

```
ng[] args) {

anner(System.in);

 number: ");

n + " is even");

n + " is odd");
```

ACTIVITIES & TOOLS

WRITE AN ALGORITHM

We use algorithms all the time. A cooking recipe is an algorithm. So are the instructions to put together a toy. In this activity, you will write an algorithm for tying shoes.

What You Need:
- paper
- pencil

❶ Imagine you are explaining step-by-step instructions for tying a shoe.

❷ On your piece of paper, make a numbered list. Write the first step for tying shoes next to number one.

❸ Continue writing steps, with each next to its own number.

❹ What is your final step? How do you know when the shoe is tied?

❺ You have just written an algorithm! Try to follow your own instructions. Are your shoes tied tight?

❻ If they are not, go back and edit your algorithm and try again.

GLOSSARY

algorithms: Sets of instructions for solving problems or completing tasks.

animations: Moving drawings, pictures, or computer graphics.

apps: Short for applications; computer programs that do specific tasks and are designed for mobile devices.

binary code: Code used in digital computers consisting of two states, on and off, which are represented by 1s and 0s.

bit: The smallest unit of storage in a computer, storing a single binary digit.

byte: A unit of storage in a computer that contains eight bits and communicates one letter or character.

circuits: Wired pathways inside computers along which electricity flows.

code: Step-by-step programming statements, written in a coding language, that tell a computer what to do.

compilers: Computer programs, or sets of programs, that change computer code written in coding languages to binary code.

computer programs: Software that runs on computers to perform particular tasks.

device: A piece of equipment that does a particular job.

programmers: People who write the code that allows computer programs to work properly.

transistors: Devices in electric circuits that switch electric signals on and off.

translated: Changed from one language to another.

JavaScript
C#
Python
Ruby
PERL
C++
HTML
PHP

INDEX

TO LEARN MORE

Finding more information is as easy as 1, 2, 3.

❶ Go to www.factsurfer.com

❷ Enter "whatiscoding?" into the search box.

❸ Choose your book to see a list of websites.

FACT SURFER